Headfirst Into Maths

Number Calculations

David Kirkby

Heinemann
LIBRARY

First published in Great Britain by Heinemann Library,
Halley Court, Jordan Hill, Oxford OX2 8EJ,
a division of Reed Educational and Professional Publishing Ltd.
Heinemann is a registered trademark of Reed Educational & Professional Publishing Limited.

OXFORD MELBOURNE AUCKLAND
JOHANNESBURG BLANTYRE GABORONE
IBADAN PORTSMOUTH NH (USA) CHICAGO

Designed by Susan Clarke
Illustrations by Sascha Lipscomb
Origination by Ambassador Litho Ltd
Printed by Wing King Tong in Hong Kong

04 03 02 01 00
10 9 8 7 6 5 4 3 2 1

ISBN 0 431 08024 0
This title is also available in a hardback library edition (ISBN 0 431 08017 8).

British Library Cataloguing in Publication Data
Kirkby, David
Number calculations. – (Head first into maths)
1.Arithmetic – Juvenile literature 2.Arithmetic – Problems,
exercises, etc. – Juvenile literature
I.Title
513

Acknowledgements
The Publishers would like to thank the following for permission to reproduce photographs:
Trevor Clifford, pp 16, 24; Hutchison Library (N. Durrell McKenna), p 4.

Our thanks to Hilary Koll and Steve Mills for their comments in the preparation of this book.

Every effort has been made to contact copyright holders of any material reproduced
in this book. Any omissions will be rectified in subsequent printings if notice is given
to the Publisher.

For more information about Heinemann Library books, or to order, please phone 01865 888055,
or send a fax to 01865 314091. You can visit our web site at www.heinemann.co.uk

Contents

Any words appearing in the text in bold, **like this**, are explained in the Glossary

Calculations

To **calculate** something means to work it out.

When you have worked something out, you have done a **calculation**.

Some calculations you do in your head – these are called mental calculations.

Many calculations are number calculations, when the working out involves numbers.

? Question
What is the total cost?

Sometimes you need to write things down to work them out. These are called written calculations.

▲ *Some people use machines to help them calculate. In countries in the Far East such as Japan and China, many people use an **abacus** to help them check calculations.*

▶ *When you go shopping, you need to do calculations. Do you have enough money? If you want to buy something that costs 63p, which coins will you pay with? How much change do you expect to be given?*

You need to be good at calculations when you go shopping.

The shopkeeper uses a till to help with her calculations. The till prints out a **receipt**. The receipt shows all the things you have bought, how much they each cost, the total bill, and the amount of change.

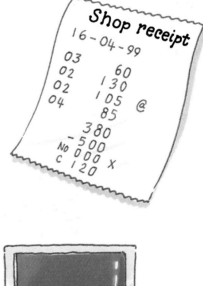

Shop receipt

16 - 04 - 99

03
02   60
02   1 30
04   1 05 @
           85
       3 80
     - 5 00
No 0 0 0 X
C 1 2 0 X

apples   60p
Potatoes £1·30
bread £1·05
Cola   85p

? Question

Can you total this bill in your head?

Many people use a hand **calculator** to help them check their calculations.

▲ *More difficult calculations can be worked out on a computer. The computer can store calculations in its memory.*

The four most common types of calculation are **adding**, **subtracting**, **multiplying** and **dividing**.

Adding

Adding means putting two or more amounts or sets of objects together. We **add** them together to work out how many there are in total.

◀ *Tom and Karen have been collecting shells. To find out how many they have between them, we add the two amounts, 7 and 5 together, making 12.*

TIP Start with the larger amount (7), and count on the smaller amount (5).

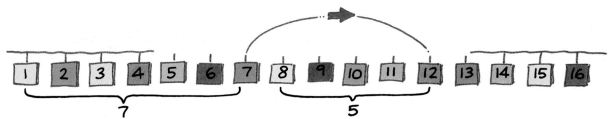

▲ *A **number line** helps. We count on along the line, or we jump forwards along the line.*
We write 7 + 5 = 12.

What does it mean?

The '+' sign reads 'add' or 'and' or '**plus**'.

The '=' sign reads 'makes' or 'is' or 'equals'.

7 + 5 = 12 is called an **addition**.

You can read it as 'seven plus five equals two'.

The answer, 12, is sometimes called the **total** of 7 and 5.

? Question

James has read page 45. If he reads anothe
32 pages, what page will he reach?

This is an addition problem: 45 + 32 = ?

TIP Start with the larger number (45),
add the **tens** (30), to make 75, then add
the **units** (2) to make 77.

1	2	3	4	5	6	7	8	9	10
11	12	13	14	15	16	17	18	19	20
21	22	23	24	25	26	27	28	29	30
31	32	33	34	35	36	37	38	39	40
41	42	43	44	45	46	47	48	49	50
51	52	53	54	55	56	57	58	59	60
61	62	63	64	65	66	67	68	69	70
71	72	73	74	75	76	77	78	79	80
81	82	83	84	85	86	87	88	89	90
91	92	93	94	95	96	97	98	99	100

◀ *A 1–100 square
helps with the addition.
Start with 45.
Add 30 : slide down 3 places.
Add 2 : slide right 2 places.
Write 45 + 32 = 77*

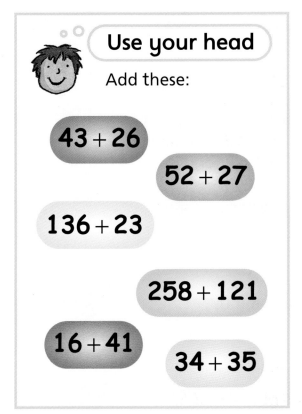

Use your head

Add these:

43 + 26

52 + 27

136 + 23

258 + 121

16 + 41

34 + 35

Play the addition game

This is a game for two players.
Choose a number to add, such
as 23. Use a book with lots of
pages. Take turns to open the
book and look at the page
number on the right, for example
34. Add 23 to the page number
to make 57. Check each other's
additions. If correct, score
points to match the units digit
of the answer, in this case,
7 points. Play several rounds.
Who scored the most points?

Subtracting

If we have a number of objects, and we take some away to see how many are left, we are subtracting. We take one amount away from another.

To take away is called to **subtract**.

? Question

Kerry is cooking breakfast. He needs 4 eggs. How many eggs will be left?

TIP Start with 12, then count back 4, leaving 8.

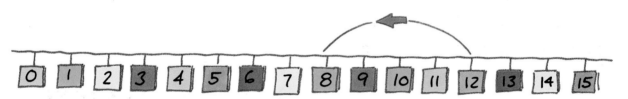

▲ *A **number line** helps. We count back along the line, or we jump backwards along the line. We write 12 – 4 = 8.*

What does it mean?

The – sign reads 'take away' or 'subtract' or '**minus**'.

The = sign reads 'leaves' or 'is' or 'equals'.

12 – 4 = 8 is called a **subtraction**. You can read it as 'twelve minus four equals eight'.

◀ *Mr Rees, the baker, baked 78 loaves of bread today. He has sold 25 already. How many loaves are still left?*

This is a subtraction problem: $78 - 25 = ?$

TIP Start with 78, take away the **tens** (20) to leave 58, then take away the **units** (5) to leave 53.

1	2	3	4	5	6	7	8	9	10
11	12	13	14	15	16	17	18	19	20
21	22	23	24	25	26	27	28	29	30
31	32	33	34	35	36	37	38	39	40
41	42	43	44	45	46	47	48	49	50
51	52	53	54	55	56	57	58	59	60
61	62	63	64	65	66	67	68	69	70
71	72	73	74	75	76	77	78	79	80
81	82	83	84	85	86	87	88	89	90
91	92	93	94	95	96	97	98	99	100

◀ *A 1–100 square helps with the subtraction.*
Start with 78.
Take away 20 : slide up 2 places.
Take away 5 : slide left 5 places.
Write 78 −25 = 53

Use your head

Try these subtractions:

$276 - 44$ $95 - 53$

$65 - 21$ $58 - 16$

$369 - 125$ $73 - 42$

Play the subtraction game

This is a game for two players. Each player starts with 100 points.

Take turns to throw three dice, and find the total. Take that total away from your points. Check each other's subtractions. Keep score. Who is the first to lose all their points?

Multiplying

Multiplying is adding several lots of the same amount.

For example, the addition 5 + 5 + 5 + 5 + 5 + 5, which is 6 lots of 5, is a **multiplication**.

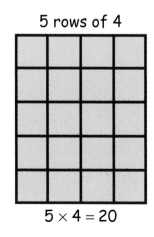

? Question

How many oranges and how many apples are there?

There are 5 rows of 4 oranges, or 5 lots of 4 oranges, or 5 fours, which is 4 + 4 + 4 + 4 + 4 = 20 oranges.

There are 3 rows of 6 apples, or 6 lots of 3 apples, or 3 sixes, which is 6 + 6 + 6 = 18 apples.

We write: $5 \times 4 = 20$

$3 \times 6 = 18$

What does it mean?

The '×' sign reads 'lots of' or 'times'.

$5 \times 4 = 20$ and $3 \times 6 = 18$ are called multiplications. You can read them as 'five times four equals twenty' and 'three times six equals eighteen'.

TIP Draw the rows (or 'lots of') on squared paper, to show the amount of fruit.

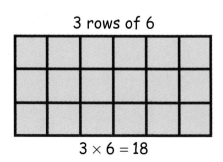

5 rows of 4

$5 \times 4 = 20$

3 rows of 6

$3 \times 6 = 18$

▶ In 1 row, there are 1 × 4 = 4 melons
In 2 rows, there are 2 × 4 = 8 melons
In 3 rows, there are 3 × 4 = 12 melons
and so on …
This produces the × 4 **multiplication table**
or times four multiplication table.

1 × 4 = 4	
2 × 4 = 8	
3 × 4 = 12	
4 × 4 = 16	
5 × 4 = 20	
6 × 4 = 24	
7 × 4 = 28	
8 × 4 = 32	
9 × 4 = 36	
10 × 4 = 40	

▶ A **multiplication square** shows all the numbers in the ×4 table in the 4th row.

Other multiplication tables are shown in the other rows.

1	2	3	4	5	6	7	8	9	10
2	4	6	8	10	12	14	16	18	20
3	6	9	12	15	18	21	24	27	30
4	8	12	16	20	24	28	32	36	40
5	10	15	20	25	30	35	40	45	50
6	12	18	24	30	36	42	48	54	60
7	14	21	28	35	42	49	56	63	70
8	16	24	32	40	48	56	64	72	80
9	18	27	36	45	54	63	72	81	90
10	20	30	40	50	60	70	80	90	100

You can use the square to check multiplications, for example for 7 × 6, look along the 7th row and down the 6th column, to find 42.

Use your head

Try these multiplications without looking at the multiplication square. Then use the square to check them.

4 × 7   6 × 9   8 × 4   3 × 8   7 × 5

Play the multiplication game

This is a game for two players. Throw two dice each and multiply the two dice numbers together. Check each other's multiplications, using the square if necessary. The player with the largest answer collects one counter. Who is the first to collect 10 counters?

Dividing

To **divide** something is to split it up into parts.

When we split an amount into equal parts it is called **division**.

? Question

The cakes are to be packed in rows of 4. How many rows of cakes will there be?

The cakes are being split up or divided into fours.

There will be 4 + 4 + 4 or three 4s to make 12.

We write: $12 \div 4 = 3$

What does it mean?

The '÷' sign reads 'divided by'.

Division is the reverse (or opposite) of **multiplication**.

Read $12 \div 4 = ?$ as 'twelve divided by four equals …', or 'how many fours make twelve?'

▶ *The children are being divided into teams of five.*

? Question

There are 30 children. How many teams will there be?
We write $30 \div 5 = ?$, and say 'how many fives make thirty?'

TIP Use the **multiplication square** to help you find how many fives make thirty.

1	2	3	4	5	6	7	8	9	10
2	4	6	8	10	12	14	16	18	20
3	6	9	12	15	18	21	24	27	30
4	8	12	16	20	24	28	32	36	40
5	10	15	20	25	30	35	40	45	50
6	12	18	24	30	36	42	48	54	60
7	14	21	28	35	42	49	56	63	70
8	16	24	32	40	48	56	64	72	80
9	18	27	36	45	54	63	72	81	90
10	20	30	40	50	60	70	80	90	100

6 fives make 30

So, $30 \div 5 = 6$

Suppose that, instead of 30 children there were 33 children.

There will be 6 teams of 5, and then 3 children left over.

The division is not exact.

The 3 left over are called the **remainder**.

So, we write $33 \div 5 = 6$ remainder 3

Use your head

Try these divisions without looking at the multiplication square. Use the square to check them.

$36 \div 4$

$14 \div 2$

$30 \div 3$

$72 \div 9$

$24 \div 6$

Play the division game

This is a game for two players. Make some cards, each with a separate division written on them, for example $12 \div 4$, $25 \div 5$, $27 \div 3$.

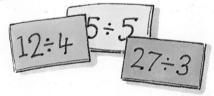

Shuffle the cards and spread them out face down. Take turns to turn over a card, and try to say the answer. If correct, keep the card. If not, return the card face down. Use the multiplication square as a check. The winner is the player who collects the most cards.

Addition pairs

The **addition** pairs to 5 are all the pairs of numbers which add to make 5:

0	1	2	3	4	5
5	4	3	2	1	0

▲ *A tower of 10 cubes can be split into two smaller towers in different ways. These show the addition pairs to 10. Knowing all the pairs to 10 makes it easier to work out more difficult* **calculations**.

These are the pairs:

0	1	2	3	4	5	6	7	8	9	10
10	9	8	7	6	5	4	3	2	1	0

Knowing the addition pairs to 60 is useful.

? Question

How many minutes are there to go
before the next hour on each clock?

Knowing the addition pairs to 100 is also useful.

They are easy when they are the **multiples** of 10
(the '**tens**'). Knowing the addition pairs to 10 helps you.

0	10	20	30	40	50	60	70	80	90	100
100	90	80	70	60	50	40	30	20	10	0

It is more difficult when the
numbers are not multiples of 10.

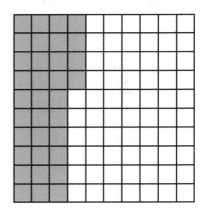

▲

34 red, 66 white
34 + 66 = 100

75p

48p

62p

30p

? Question

How much change is there from £1 for each of these items?

TIP   Imagine the amount coloured on a 10 × 10 square.

Doubling

What does it mean?

The **double** of an amount is two lots of the amount.

Two lots of an amount is called **twice** the amount.

Double 10 is 10 + 10 = 20

◀ *These are doubles.*

▶ *Darts in the outer ring score double points.*
Double 4 is 4 + 4 = 8

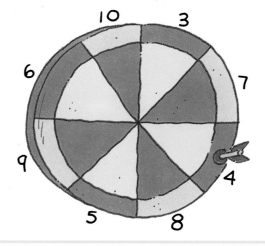

Use your head

Say the total score on each dartboard.

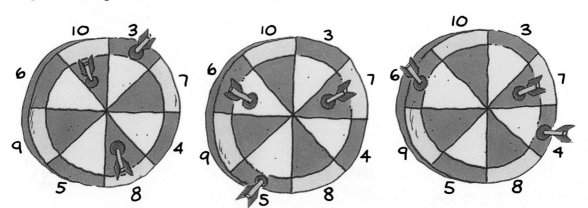

▶ *When a number is fed into the doubling machine, out comes its double.*

Doubling is easy when you know the doubles of:

- the numbers 1 to 10
- the 'tens': 10, 20, 30, …

IN	number	1	2	3	4	5	6	7	8	9	10
OUT	double	2	4	6	8	10	12	14	16	18	20

TIP To double 24:

- double the tens
- double the units
- add together.

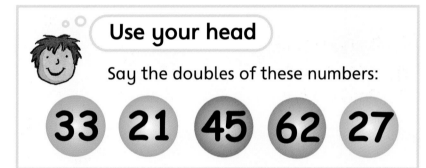

Use your head

Say the doubles of these numbers:

33 21 45 62 27

Play the doubling game

This is a game for two players. Start by writing all the doubles up to 50 to make a game board. Use several dice and two sets of counters of different colours, one colour for each player. When it is your turn, choose to throw as many dice as you like, find the total, then double it. If the answer appears on the board, cover it with one of your counters. Continue until all the doubles are covered. The winner is the player who covered the most.

Halving and doubling

To find a **half** of something, you split it into two, or **divide** it by 2.

Halving is the reverse (or opposite) of doubling.

If **double** 12 is 24, then half of 24 is 12.

▲ *If you know the number which comes out of the doubling machine, halve it to find the number which went into the machine.*

? Question

These are the old prices. The shop is selling **everything at half the old price. How much do you need to pay for each item?**

Half-price

28p

66p

60p

42p

82p

Doubling can be used to make calculations easier.

  ? **Question**
What is the total of these points?

You can use doubles to add.

TIP Match the **addition** to a near double.

8 + 9 is near double 8 : then add 1 $16 + 1 = 17$

or 8 + 9 is near double 9 : then take 1 away $18 - 1 = 17$

 Use your head

Use near doubles to find these totals:

$14 + 15$ $23 + 24$ $51 + 52$ $7 + 8$ $32 + 33$

Play the halving and doubling game

This a game for two players.
You need two dice.

Take turns to throw the dice,
and find the total score.

If the total is **odd**, double it.

If the total is **even**, halve it.

Make a score sheet like this and fill
in your scores.

The winner is the player with the
highest total score after 8 rounds.

Play another game, this time using
3 dice or maybe 4 dice.

Round	Kim	Stephen
1		
2		
3		
4		
5		
6		
7		
8		
total		

Tips to help you add

Sometimes there are short cuts to help you **add**.

? **Question**

What is the **total** of each set of cards?

TIP   Look for a pair which makes 10, then add the others.

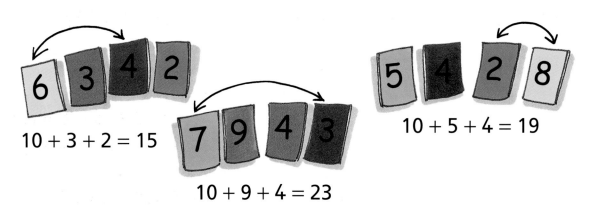

$10 + 3 + 2 = 15$

$10 + 9 + 4 = 23$

$10 + 5 + 4 = 19$

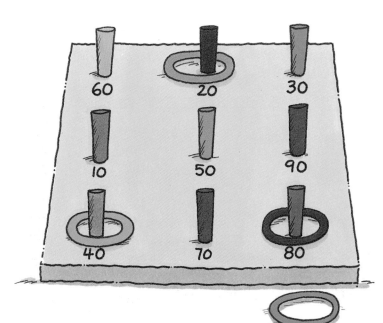

? **Question**

What is the total score?

TIP   Look for a pair which makes 100.

$20 + 80 + 40 = 140$

❓ Question

What is the total cost of sending each letter?

TIP To add 9, first add 10, then take away 1.

$10 + 7 = 17$ $13 + 10 = 23$ $10 + 26 = 36$

$17 - 1 = 16p$ $23 - 1 = 22p$ $36 - 1 = 35p$

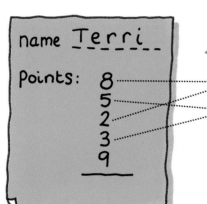

name Terri

Points: 8
         5
         2
         3
         9

◀ *What is the total score?*

Spot the pair to 10 (2 and 8 = 10)

Add the little bits (5 and 3 = 8)

Spot the 9

Total is $18 + 9 = 28 - 1 = 27$

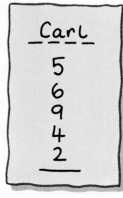

Use your head

What are these total scores?

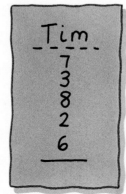

Carl	Tim	Sue	Katie
5	7	5	4
6	3	9	2
9	8	5	19
4	2	4	7
2	6	2	6

Tips to help you subtract

If two amounts have a **difference** of 3, then one amount is 3 more than the other. This is the same as saying one amount is 3 less than the other.

▲ *The difference between the towers is 3. One is 3 cubes taller than the other, one is 3 cubes shorter than the other.*

TIP To find a difference, imagine a **number line**.

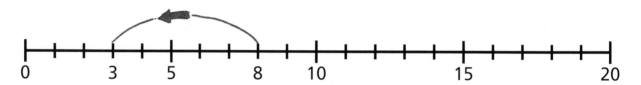

One way to find a difference between 5 and 8 is to **subtract**: $8 - 5$

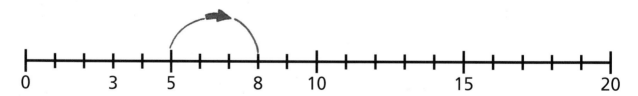

Another way is to **add**: $5 + ? = 8$

? **Question**

? Question

What is the difference between these two amounts of money?

One way is to subtract: $72 - 29$

Another way is to find what must be added to the smaller number 29 to make the larger number 72, by counting on.

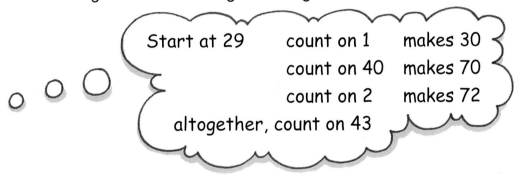

Start at 29   count on 1   makes 30

count on 40   makes 70

count on 2   makes 72

altogether, count on 43

So $72 - 29 = 43$

TIP To find the difference, imagine the number line:

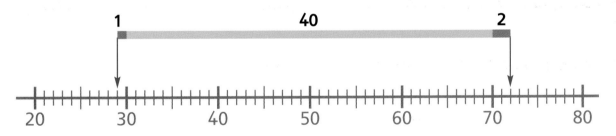

? Question

Can you say the difference between the lengths of each pair?

23

Tips to help you multiply

◀ *Numbers to be **multiplied** can be swapped round. The result is the same. 4 × 5 and 5 × 4 both make 20.*

TIP If you are not sure what five sevens (5 × 7) are, for example, try swapping it round to seven fives (7 × 5).

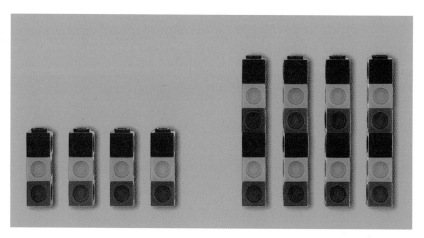

▲ *Six is **double** three. Sets of sixes are double sets of threes. 4 × 3 = 12. Double 12 is 24, so, 4 × 6 = 24*

TIP Use doubling to help you multiply.

The ×3 table	The ×6 table
1 × 3 = 3	1 × 6 = 6
2 × 3 = 6	2 × 6 = 12
3 × 3 = 9	3 × 6 = ?
4 × 3 = 12	4 × 6 = ?
5 × 3 = 15	5 × 6 = ?
...	...

TIP Use the × 6 row to help you multiply by 12.

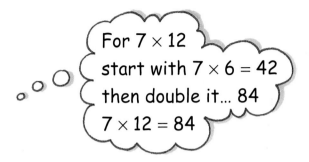

For 7 × 12 start with 7 × 6 = 42 then double it... 84 7 × 12 = 84

1	2	3	4	5	6	7	8	9	10
2	4	6	8	10	12	14	16	18	20
3	6	9	12	15	18	21	24	27	30
4	8	12	16	20	24	28	32	36	40
5	10	15	20	25	30	35	40	45	50
6	12	18	24	30	36	42	48	54	60
7	14	21	28	35	42	49	56	63	70
8	16	24	32	40	48	56	64	72	80
9	18	27	36	45	54	63	72	81	90
10	20	30	40	50	60	70	80	90	100

1	2	3	4	5	6	7	8	9	10
2	4	6	8	10	12	14	16	18	20
3	6	9	12	15	18	21	24	27	30
4	8	12	16	20	24	28	32	36	40
5	10	15	20	25	30	35	40	45	50
6	12	18	24	30	36	42	48	54	60
7	14	21	28	35	42	49	56	63	70
8	16	24	32	40	48	56	64	72	80
9	18	27	36	45	54	63	72	81	90
10	20	30	40	50	60	70	80	90	100

◀ *Double the 2s for the 4s.*
Double the 4s for the 8s.

? **Question**

How many candles altogether? Use doubling.

Multiplying by 10 and by 100

? Question

Jasmine has 17 crayons. They cost 10p each. How much did the crayons cost altogether?

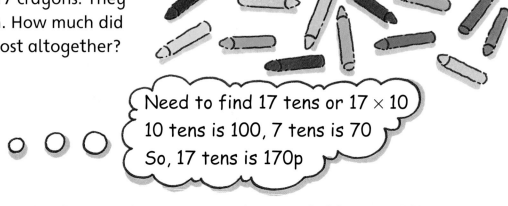

Need to find 17 tens or 17 × 10

10 tens is 100, 7 tens is 70

So, 17 tens is 170p

TIP Imagine the **digits** in their correct columns. Th (thousands), H (hundreds), T (tens), U (units), t (tenths).

To **multiply** by 10, slide all the digits one place to the left.

Th	H	T	U	t
		1	7	

$\times 10 \rightarrow$

Th	H	T	U	t
	1	7	0	

Use your head

Say how much each of these boxes of crayons cost if each crayon costs 10p.

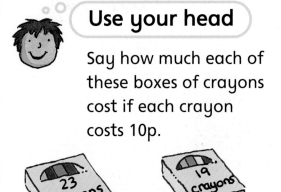

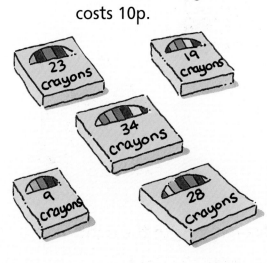

23 crayons

19 crayons

34 crayons

9 crayons

28 crayons

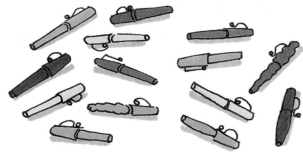

? Question

Each pen cost 20p. How much did they cost altogether?

TIP To multiply by 20, ... **double** first, then multiply by 10.

14 × 20? ... double 14 = 28

28 × 10 = 280p

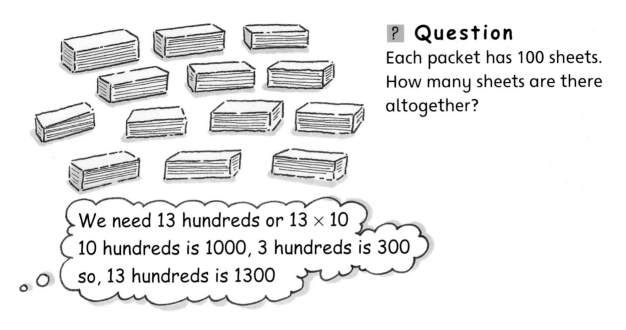

Each packet has 100 sheets.
How many sheets are there
altogether?

We need 13 hundreds or 13 × 10
10 hundreds is 1000, 3 hundreds is 300
so, 13 hundreds is 1300

TIP To multiply by 100,
slide all the digits two places
to the left.

Th	H	T	U	t
		1	3	

× 100 →

Th	H	T	U	t
1	3	0	0	

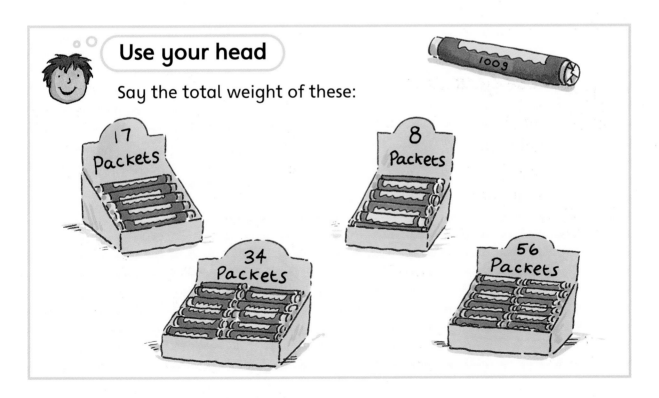

Use your head

Say the total weight of these:

17 Packets

8 Packets

34 Packets

56 Packets

TIP To **divide** by 10, slide all the digits one place to the right.

To divide by 100 slide all the digits two places to the right.

Written calculations

When the numbers that you need to add become larger, it is more difficult to **add** 'in your head' using a mental **calculation**. You can write the **addition** on paper using a written method.

❓ Question

What is the total weight of the boxes?

This is an addition problem: **238 + 145 = ?**

Written Method 1	
	238
	+ 145
add the hundreds first	300
add the tens	70
add the units	13
then add each column	383

Written Method 2	
	238
	+ 145
add the units first	13
add the tens	70
add the hundreds	300
then add each column	383

Written Method 3	
	238 + 145
start with 238	238
+ 100	= 338
+ 40	= 378
+ 5	= 383

There are always lots of different written methods for adding. Which do you like best?

You also need written methods for more difficult **multiplications**. One way is to draw a picture of rectangles.

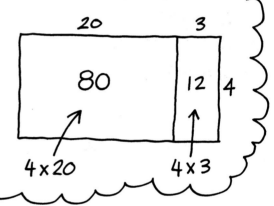

? **Question**

I need 4 more stickers for my collection. How much will they cost me?

I need to calculate 4×23

TIP

Draw a 4×23 rectangle.

Imagine the 23 split into tens and units.

Split the rectangle into parts.

Multiply for each part.

Add the parts together.

	20	3
	80	12	4

4×20 4×3

The cost of 4 stickers is 92p.

$80 + 12 = 92.$

What would be the price of 35 stickers at the same price?

You need to calculate 35×23

TIP

Draw a 35×23 rectangle.

Imagine the 23 and the 35 split into tens and units.

Split the rectangle into parts.

Multiply for each part.

Add the parts together.

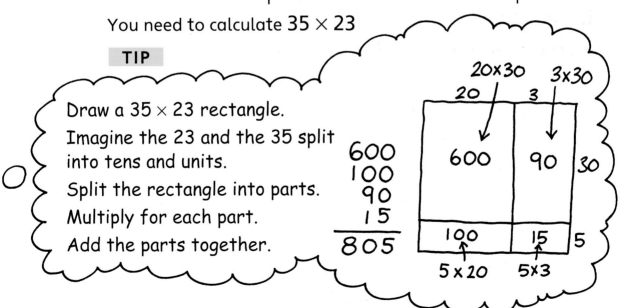

$$\begin{array}{r} 600 \\ 100 \\ 90 \\ 15 \\ \hline 805 \end{array}$$

The cost of 35 stickers is 805p or £8·05

Glossary

abacus	a piece of apparatus to show numbers and to calculate with numbers
add/adding	put two or more objects or numbers together and count the total
addition	what you are doing when you add
calculate	to work something out
calculation	process or result of working something out
calculator	electronic device that calculates (works out) sums
difference	the difference between two numbers is how much more one is than the other
digit	a symbol, 0 to 9, used to write a number
divide	to split something up into equal parts
division	what you are doing when you divide
double	double a number is two times the number
even number	a whole number which can be divided exactly by 2
half	something divided into two equal parts
minus	a sign for subtract or take away, '−'
multiple	a number that is in a times table. Multiples of 3 are 3, 6, 9, 12, ...
multiply	find several lots of the same amount
multiplication	what you are doing when you multiply
multiplication square	a 10 by 10 square showing the results of all the multiplication facts up to 10×10
multiplication table	a list showing the multiples of a number. For the times 4 table the list shows the multiples of 4.
number line	a line with 'divisions' or markings which are numbered in order
odd number	a whole number which is not even

plus	a sign for add, '+'
remainder	the amount left over when a division is not exact
receipt	a list to show the things you have bought and how much they cost
subtract	take some objects away from a set of objects and count how many are left
subtraction	what you are doing when you subtract
tens	in a number such as 129, the number second from the right (2) tells us how many tens we have
total	the answer you get by adding numbers together
twice	two times
units	in a number such as 129, the digit on the right (9) tells us how many ones we have

Answers

Page 4
<u>Question</u>
67p

Page 5
<u>Question</u>
£3.80

Page 7
<u>Use your head</u>
$43 + 26 = 69$;
$52 + 27 = 79$;
$136 + 23 = 159$;
$258 + 121 = 379$;
$16 + 41 = 57$;
$34 + 35 = 69$

Page 9
<u>Use your head</u>
$276 - 44 = 232$; $95 - 53 = 42$;
$65 - 21 = 44$; $58 - 16 = 42$;
$369 - 125 = 244$; $73 - 42 = 31$

Page 11
<u>Use your head</u>
$4 \times 7 = 28$; $6 \times 9 = 54$;
$8 \times 4 = 32$; $3 \times 8 = 24$;
$7 \times 5 = 35$

Page 13
<u>Use your head</u>
$36 \div 4 = 9$; $14 \div 2 = 7$;
$30 \div 3 = 10$; $72 \div 9 = 8$;
$24 \div 6 = 4$

Page 15
<u>Question</u>
07:40: 20 minutes;
05:25: 35 minutes;
06:28: 32 minutes;
08:33: 27 minutes
<u>Question</u>
75p: 25p change;
48p: 52p change;
30p: 70p change;
62p: 38p change

Page 16
<u>Use your head</u>
24; 23; 27

Page 17
<u>Use your head</u>
66; 42; 90; 124; 54

Page 18
<u>Question</u>
28p:14p; 66p: 33p; 60p: 30p;
42p: 21p; 82p: 41p;

Page 19
<u>Use your head</u>
$14 + 15 = 29$; $23 + 24 = 47$;
$51 + 52 = 103$; $7 + 8 = 15$;
$32 + 33 = 65$

Page 21
<u>Use your head</u>
Carl: 26: Tim: 26; Sara: 25;
Katie: 38

Page 23
<u>Question</u>
$64cm - 28cm = 36cm$;
$56cm - 19cm = 37cm$;
$62cm - 37cm = 25cm$

Page 25
<u>Question</u>
64

Page 26
<u>Use your head</u>
230p; 190p; 340p; 90p; 280p

Page 27
<u>Use your head</u>
1700 grams; 3400 grams;
800 grams; 5600 grams

Index